Qingdao
Grand Theater
in China

The Qingdao
Grand Theater
in China

Meinhard von Gerkan
Stephan Schütz

Qingdao Grand Theater in China

The Qingdao Grand Theater in China

jovis

gmp · Architekten von Gerkan, Marg und Partner

Verortung

Location

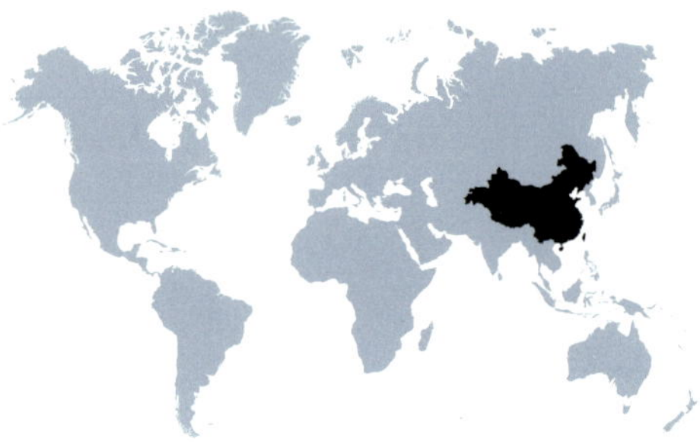

36° 5′ N, 120° 20′ O

Qingdao

Die traditionsreiche Bade- und Hafenstadt in der Provinz Shandong ist an drei Seiten vom Gelben Meer umgeben. Aufgrund seiner guten geografischen Lage entwickelte sich Qingdao seit Ende des 19. Jahrhunderts zum Handelsstützpunkt. Die deutschen Einflüsse erkennt man zum Beispiel an dem weltbekannten Tsingtao-Bier, welches dort nach deutschem Reinheitsgebot gebraut wird. Ebenso sind in dem heutigen Stadtbild der 8,5 Millionen Metropole noch einige nach deutschem Vorbild gebaute Gebäude erkennbar. Stolz bekennt man sich in Qingdao zu seinen historisch gewachsenen internationalen Beziehungen.

Geografisch liegt Qingdao zwischen dem malerischen, 1133 Meter hohen Laoshan-Gebirge und den breiten Stränden des Gelben Meeres. Mit dieser Kulisse überrascht es nicht, dass die in Deutschland als „das Neapel am Gelben Meer" bekannte Stadt einer der beliebtesten Badeorte im „Reich der Mitte" ist. So wurden 2008 auch die olympischen Segelwettbewerbe in der Fushanbucht ausgetragen. Mit seinem Tiefseehafen ist Qingdao der drittgrößte Hafen Chinas, was der Stadt eine entsprechende wirtschaftliche Kraft verleiht.

Qingdao

One of China's most popular seaside resorts and the nation's third largest harbor city overlooks the Yellow Sea on three sides. Due to its outstanding geographical location, Qingdao has been a busy trading post since the end of 19th century. International influences can also be detected: for example, the world famous Tsingtao-beer is brewed there according to the German beer brewing tradition. Furthermore, the city center is adorned by quite a few buildings that emulate indigenous German architecture. Qingdao has grown into a metropolis of 8.5 million, which is still proud of its historical, cultural, and architectural heritage.

Geographically, Qingdao is situated between the picturesque, 1,133-meter-high Laoshan mountain range and the wide beaches of the Yellow Sea. It is therefore no surprise that in Germany, China's seaside resort is praised as the "Naples on the Yellow Sea". In 2008, the Olympic sailing competitions were held in the bay of Fushan. Economically, it is the deep water harbor that bestows an even greater significance and power to Qingdao than its cultural heritage.

Peking Beijing
Qingdao
China
Shanghai

Vorwort

Meinhard von Gerkan

Kulturbauten prägen das Gesicht unserer Städte, sie schaffen Unverwechselbarkeit und Identität. Durch diese primäre Stellung im urbanen Kontext stellen sie in besonderem Maße Orte der öffentlichen Begegnung und des städtischen Diskurses dar. Für uns Architekten stellt die Planung von Kulturbauten in zweifacher Hinsicht eine besondere Herausforderung dar: Kulturbauten, insbesondere Theater- und Konzertgebäude, reflektieren historische, gesellschaftliche und kulturelle Bezüge und erschaffen auf diese Weise den Genius Loci einer Stadt. Die geblähten Segel des Opernhauses in Sydney von Jørn Utzon gehören für mich bis heute zu den eindrucksvollsten architektonischen Monumenten, die durch ihre metaphorische Überhöhung eine ganze Stadt weltberühmt gemacht haben.

Gleichermaßen geht es bei Theaterbauten um die Schaffung von Stadträumen, die Menschen einladen, sich zwanglos zu treffen. In dieser Symbiose von ikonografischer Inszenierung einerseits und öffentlicher Bedeutung andererseits stellen Theaterbauten eine herausragende Aufgabenstellung dar.

Es ist sicherlich nicht verwunderlich, dass im Kontext der rapiden Urbanisierung Chinas dem Bautypus des Theaters eine extrem wichtige Rolle zukommt. In ihm manifestieren sich wahrnehmbare Unterschiede der ansonsten oft gesichtslosen Städte. China ist ein Land der Experimente und der Visionen. Es gibt in China aufgrund der allerorten wahrnehmbaren Aufbruchstimmung unzählige Bauaufgaben im kulturellen Bereich, mit denen man in Europa heutzutage kaum noch konfrontiert ist. Allein in China haben wir drei „Grand Theaters" in den chinesischen Metropolen Tianjin, Chongqing und Qingdao realisiert. Diese „Musiktheater" sind wesentlich komplexer als europäische Opernhäuser und stellen eine in China typische Kombination verschiedener eigenständiger Bühnen für Opernaufführungen, Konzerte und Veranstaltungen in einem einzigen Gebäude dar. Nicht selten sind Museen, Hotels und Konferenzzentren integriert und werden zum beliebten Treffpunkt, zur städtischen Bühne. Diese Kulturbauten, die einen hohen gestalterischen und öffentlichen Anspruch zu erfüllen haben, stehen auf der höchsten Stufe des kulturellen Interesses im Bereich der Architektur. Sie werden damit auch von breiten Bevölkerungsschichten sowie der Fachwelt außerhalb Chinas wahrgenommen. Andererseits bringen wir dem Land eine Architektur, die sich auf Sinnfälligkeit, gute Funktion, nachhaltige Strukturen, eine Einfachheit in der Gestaltung konzentriert, auf gestalterische Attitüden verzichtet, dafür aber beste Bedingungen für Verweilqualität, für die Arbeitsplätze oder für das Kulturvergnügen bietet. Es ist eine Architektur, die sich innerhalb des zeitgenössischen Geschehens in China heute noch sehr deutlich abhebt und als ein Phänomen einer besonderen Entwicklung hin zu einer neuen Einfachheit und Reduktion einerseits sehr hochgeschätzt, natürlich gleichermaßen von anderer Seite auch stark kritisiert wird. Architektur ist eine Kunst, nach meiner Auffassung, im Gegensatz zu dem vor 30 Jahren noch verbreitetem Verständnis, dass Architektur eigentlich nur die Schaffung von Behausung ist und mit Kunst nichts zu tun habe. Und das, was in der Vergangenheit an künstlerischen Momenten sich manifestiert habe, eher nur eine gesellschaftliche Ausprägung in ganz bestimmten kulturellen Bereichen gewesen sei. Das sehe ich nicht so. Für mich ist jede Architektur, auch die oder gerade die einfache, eine Kunst. Aber, der wesentliche Unterschied zu allen, wirklich zu allen Künsten, ist der, dass es eine Kunst in der sozialen Bindung, der sozialen Anwendung ist.

Architektur entsteht immer bezogen auf menschliche Bedürfnisse. Menschliche Bedürfnisse des Wohnens, menschliche Bedürfnisse des sich Ausbildens, des Arbeitens, der Freizeitgestaltung oder kultureller Genüsse.

Architektur ist in der technologisch-zivilisierten Hemisphäre die letzte menschliche Hervorbringung, die nicht als Massenprodukt in großen Serien und damit gleicher Gestalt entsteht - sieht man von Fertighäusern ab. Man mag die bis heute nicht erreichte Industrialisierung des Bauens beklagen, weil das Bauen dadurch im Vergleich zu allen anderen Produkten unverhältnismäßig teuer ist und teurer wird. Wir sehen hierin den unschätzbaren Vorteil, mit der Architektur ein letztes Reservat zur Schaffung von Identität zu bewahren, von spezifischer Individualität, die sich aus dem entwerferischen Dialog mit jeder Aufgabe neu entwickelt, aus den Bedingungen des Ortes, des Klimas, der Nutzung, des Umfeldes gleichermaßen wie aus den Bedingungen von Konstruktion und Ökonomie. Wir sehen in dieser Chance zugleich eine verantwortungsvolle Verpflichtung für unser Tun, Orte, Lebensräume und bauliche Gestalten mit Identität zu schaffen. Für uns muss jedes Haus ein eigenes Gesicht haben, das seinen Charakter, der sich aus dem Dialog mit den Bedingungen entwickelt hat, widerspiegelt und ausdrückt.

Preface

Meinhard von Gerkan

Cultural venue buildings have an impact on the face of our cities; they create uniqueness and identity. In that prominent role in the urban context, these buildings are predestined to be places where the public can meet and where urban interaction can take place. For us architects, the design of cultural venues presents a special challenge in two ways: cultural venue buildings–theaters and concert halls in particular–reflect historic social and cultural references, and in that way create the genius loci of a city. For me, the Sydney Opera House by Jørn Utzon, with its billowing sails, to this day is one of the most impressive architectural monuments that, with its outstanding metaphoric impact, has made the entire city world-famous.

At the same time, theater buildings need to create urban spaces that invite people to meet in an informal way. In this dual role as iconographic monuments on the one hand and public meeting spaces on the other, theater buildings present an outstanding design challenge.

It is therefore not surprising that theater buildings play an extremely important role in the context of China's rapid urbanization. The addition of such buildings creates notable differences in the otherwise often faceless cities. China is a country of experiments and visions. Owing to the general atmosphere of development and change, there are numerous building projects in the cultural sphere–something that rarely arises in Europe these days. In China alone, we have completed three "Grand Theaters" in the Chinese cities of Tianjin, Chongqing, and Qingdao. These "music theaters" are much more complex than European opera houses, and involve a combination–typical for China–of different independent stages for the performance of operas, concerts, and events in a single building. In addition, museums, hotels, and conference centers are quite often integrated and become a popular meeting point, an urban stage. In terms of cultural interest in architecture, these cultural venue buildings–which have to fulfill ambitious stylistic and public purposes–fall into the top register of architectural design. As such, they are also noticed by a large proportion of the population, as well as by the professional media outside of China. On the other hand, we are introducing architecture based on a naturally confident understanding, good functionality, sustainable structures, simplicity in design and one that avoids eclectic design attitudes in favor of creating excellent and convivial environments for people to meet, to work, or to enjoy cultural events. It is an architecture that, in the context of contemporary developments in China, still clearly breaks with tradition and, as a phenomenon of a fairly unique move towards simplicity and reduction, is highly appreciated by some but naturally also heavily criticized by others. In my view architecture is an art; this view contrasts with that still popular about thirty years ago–that architecture really only meant the creation of buildings, and had nothing to do with art. And that the artistic aspects produced in the past were just the result of the social environment in very specific cultural spheres. I don't see it that way. For me, every type of architecture, including–or especially–the simplest, is art. However, the important difference between architecture and all other forms of art is that it is an art with a social purpose, with a social responsibility.

Architecture is always related to human needs–the human need for housing, the human need for learning, working, leisure pursuits, and cultural entertainment.

In the technologically civilized hemisphere, architecture is the last human creation that is not made as a mass product in large series, and hence in an identical form–except for prefabricated buildings. Some people may bemoan the fact that construction has still not been industrialized because it means that, compared to other products, buildings are disproportionally expensive and are becoming even more so. We see in this an inestimable advantage in that architecture preserves a last vestige for the creation of an identity, of a specific individuality that develops anew from the design dialogue involved in every project, from the local conditions, the climate, the type of use, the surrounding area, as well as from the constraints arising from the construction and commercial conditions. We see this as an opportunity, a responsibility, and an obligation to create living spaces and built environments for human activity that have their own identity. For us, all buildings must have their own face and their own character resulting from a dialogue reflecting and expressing the input conditions.

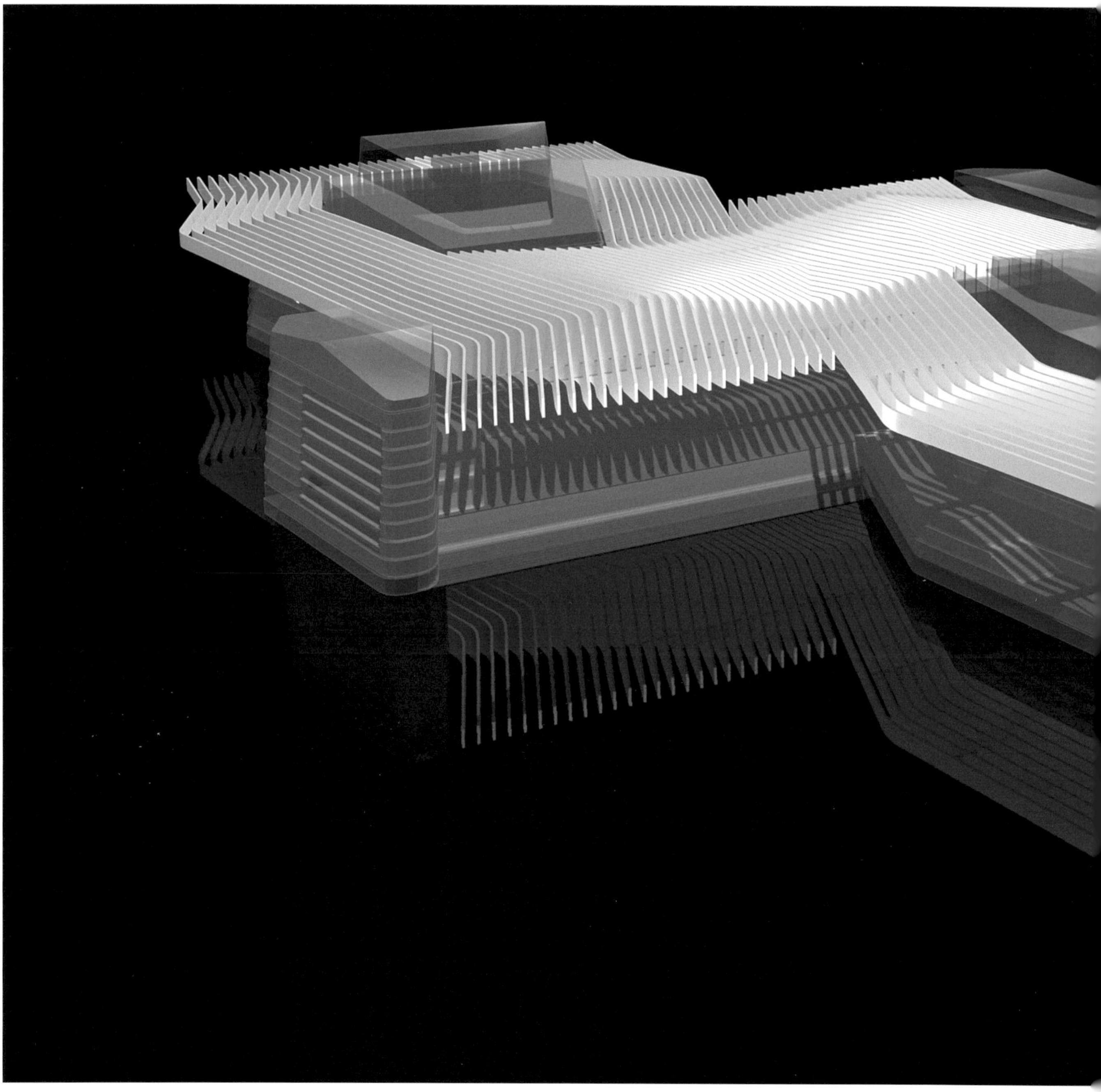

Digitales Modell des „Wolkendaches". Die Spannweite beträgt bis zu 60 Meter; die einzelnen Lamellen weisen eine Konstruktionshöhe von 6 Meter auf, die sich zum Dachrand auf eine Höhe von 2 Meter reduziert.
Digital model of the "cloud roof". The span of the roof extends up to 60 meters; its vertical panels are up to 6 meters high, reducing to 2 meters at the edge of the roof.

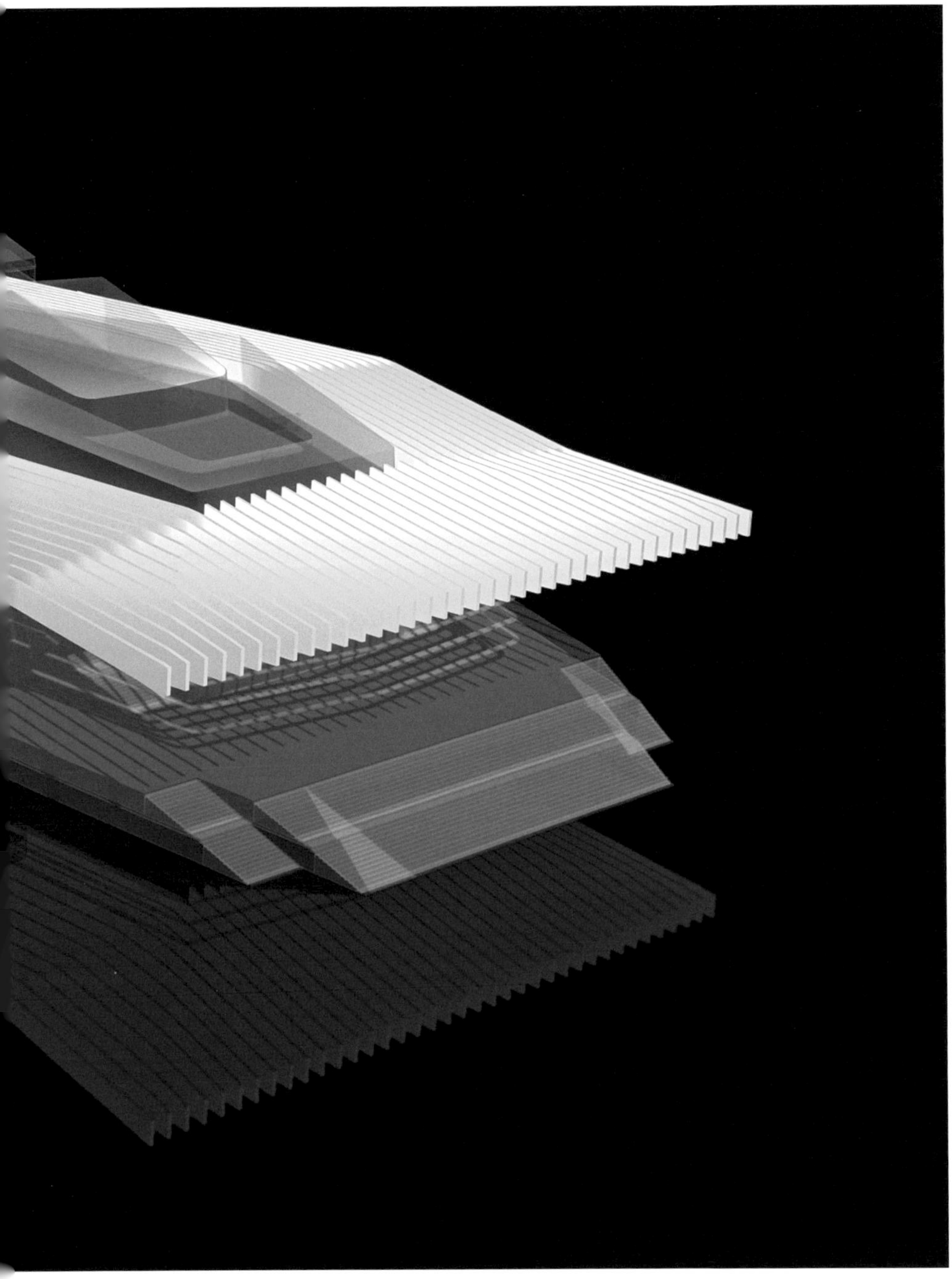

Grand Theater Qingdao – eine Bühne städtischen Lebens

Stephan Schütz
Nicolas Pomränke

Oft beschränkt sich die Grundstücksbesichtigung im Rahmen eines Wettbewerb-Kolloquiums in China auf die Begehung eines leeren Ackers, der von sehr breiten Straßen mit bereits fertiggestelltem Grünstreifen umgeben ist. Das Aufspüren des Genius Loci fällt hier meist schwer. Anders jedoch beim Wettbewerb für das Grand Theater in Qingdao. Das Grundstück liegt im Osten der Stadt, einem neuen Entwicklungsgebiet, das die auf einer Halbinsel eingezwängte Altstadt erweitert. Auch wenn die bauliche Umgebung wenig inspirierend war, so hat der Ort doch einen besonderen landschaftlichen Reiz. Das leicht nach Süden abfallende Gelände öffnet sich zum nahegelegenen Meer und wird im Norden durch ein Bergmassiv begrenzt; für chinesische Vorstellungen ein idealer Ort zum Bauen.

Das Laoshan-Massiv, das sich unmittelbar hinter dem Grundstück auf über 1000 Meter erhebt, ist ein wichtiger Bezugspunkt für die Stadt. Durch das abrupte Ansteigen des Massivs aus dem Meer sind die charakteristisch geformten Gipfel oft mit Wolken verhangen: ein Bild, das fest in der kulturellen Tradition der Stadt verankert ist. Dieses war Ausgangspunkt des Entwurfs: die Baukörper als Bergmassiv und ein filigranes Dach, das die Wolken symbolisiert. Anstatt einen kompakten Baukörper zu entwerfen, wollten wir vielmehr eine architektonische Landschaft entwickeln, die sich aus mehreren Gipfeln, Plateaus und Wegen zusammensetzt. So entstand ein Baukörper, der in seiner Gesamtheit nur in der Bewegung zu erfassen ist und so der Erfahrung einer Landschaft gleichkommt. Die großen Freitreppen stellen repräsentative Zugänge dar, aber zahlreiche Nebenwege erlauben die Erschließung der Spielstätten auf abwechslungsreiche Weise. Der breite zentrale Durchgang über das gemeinsame Podium verbindet hierbei die Berglandschaft im Norden mit dem Meer im Süden.

Es ging darum, nicht nur die internen Veranstaltungsorte zu realisieren, sondern das gesamte Gebäude zu einer Bühne städtischen Lebens zu machen. So ist das gesamte Gelände öffentlich und wird auch von Bürgern, die keine Vorstellung besuchen wollen, als Treffpunkt wahrgenommen, wobei die verschatteten Sitzplätze auf den großen Freitreppen zu Logen mit Meerblick werden.

Die durch die zentrale Durchwegung entstehende Trennung in zwei Hauptbaukörper führt hierbei zu keinerlei funktionalen Einschränkungen, vielmehr ist der seperate Zugang zu den Spielstätten von allen Seiten jederzeit gegeben. Dadurch, dass sich die Foyers der Säle auf dem Niveau des Podiums befinden, ist eine interne Verbindung im Erdgeschossniveau möglich. Zahlreiche Nebenfunktionen wie Anlieferung, Probesäle, aber auch Restaurants und Konferenzbereiche werden so funktional mit den Spielstätten verbunden. Als eigenständige Baukörper sind auch ein Hotel und ein Instrumentenmuseum über den Sockel angebunden.

Das zentrale architektonische Element ist das strahlend weiße „Wolkendach", das an seiner breitesten Stelle eine Weite von über 60 Meter überspannt. Die einzelnen Lamellen weisen eine Konstruktionshöhe von 6 Metern auf. Sie verjüngen sich zu den Rändern hin und werden vom Betrachter nicht in ihrer eigentlichen Dimension wahrgenommen. Vielmehr erzeugen die Lamellen durch den Wechsel des Sonnenstandes einen komplexen Raum, der als Übergang zwischen Stadt, Landschaft und Kultur dient.

Grand Theater Qingdao – A Stage for Urban Life

Stephan Schütz
Nicolas Pomränke

Very often, when a site is visited for the purpose of participating in a briefing meeting for a competition in China, the site consists of not much more than a green field surrounded by very wide roads complete with green strips. In such a situation, it is usually difficult to discover a distinctive genius loci. It was different, however, with the competition for the Qingdao Grand Theater. The site is situated in a new development area to the east of the city, enabling the old city to be expanded from its confined location on a peninsula. Even though little inspiration was to be gained from the existing built environment, the landscape of the place has a distinct attraction. The terrain slopes slightly towards the south opening up to the nearby sea and, to the north, is confined by a mountain range; an ideal place for building according to Chinese thought.

The Laoshan range, which rises up to over 1,000 meters behind the site, is an important reference for the city. Due to the mountain range's location directly by the sea, the characteristically shaped peaks are often shrouded in cloud – an image that is firmly anchored in the cultural tradition of the city. This was the starting point of the design, which conceived of the buildings themselves as the mountain range, with a filigree roof to symbolize the clouds. Instead of designing a solid building form, we wanted to develop a landscape with several peaks, plateaus and pathways. In this way, we created an ensemble that cannot be fully comprehended except through movement, and thus it is similar to the way we experience a landscape. The large open-air flights of steps create prestigious access routes in addition to the numerous smaller paths, which provide access to the theaters in a diverse and interesting way. A wide central passage via the shared platform connects the mountain landscape to the north with the sea to the south.

One of our main objectives was not only to provide accommodation for the internal venues, but to make the entire development into a stage for urban life. For this reason, the entire building is open to the public and is also frequented by citizens who do not want to attend a performance, with the shaded seating areas on the large open flights of steps offering views over the sea.

The separation of the development into two main parts resulting from the central passageway does not entail any functional restriction; quite the opposite is the case – the theaters can be accessed from all sides at any time. As the theater foyers are located at the platform level, an internal connection has been created at ground floor level. In this way numerous secondary functions – such as deliveries, rehearsal rooms, restaurants and conference area – are functionally linked with the theaters. The platform also provides a link to two independent buildings – a hotel and an instrument museum.

The central architectural element is the brilliant white "cloud roof" which, at its widest opening, has a span of over sixty meters. However, the depth of the structure – which reaches six meters at its deepest – is not noticeable, as the roof thickness diminishes at the edges. Owing to the change in the position of the sun, the vertical panels of the roof create a complex play of shadow and light underneath – a space that serves as a transition between city, landscape, and culture.

Im westlichen Baukörper befindet sich das Opernhaus mit 1600 Sitzplätzen und modernster Technik auf Haupt- und Nebenbühnen. Die große Freitreppe öffnet sich nach Süden zum Meer und innerhalb des „Berges" schimmert abends das festliche Rot des Saales. Dieser orientiert sich an klassischen europäischen Opernhäusern, in denen die zahlreiche Ränge das Parkett hufeisenförmig umgeben. Hierbei übernimmt die plastische Verkleidung aus farbigen Betonpaneelen komplexe akustische Anforderungen. Der östliche Baukörper nimmt den Konzertsaal und die Multifunktionshalle auf. Die Positionierung „Rücken an Rücken" erlaubt es, Anlieferung und Garderoben gemeinsam zu nutzen. Auch der Konzertsaal für 1200 Personen genügt höchsten akustischen Anforderungen. Der rombenförmige Saal teilt sich in ein geschwungenes Parkett aus warmen Ulmenholz und den Wand- und Deckenbereich, die in klarem Weiß gestaltet sind. Auch hier übernimmt die plastische, wellenförmige Ausbildung der Bauteile akustische Funktionen.

In allen Spielstätten ziehen sich die Außenfassaden in die Foyerbereiche und auch das Wolkendach setzt sich in lamellenförmigen Lichtbändern fort, sodass die Grenzen zwischen Innen und Außen verschwimmen: Der Spaziergang durch die Landschaft des Laoshan-Gebirges setzt sich im Inneren fort.

The Opera House, with its 1,600 seats and state-of-the-art technology serving its main and secondary stages, is situated in the western part of the building. The large open-air flight of steps opens up to the sea to the south, and within the "mountain", the festive red of the auditorium shimmers at night. The auditorium replicates the design of classic European opera houses, with numerous balconies surrounding the stalls in the shape of a horseshoe. The sculptural cladding with colored concrete panels fulfills complex acoustic requirements.

The eastern part of the building accommodates the concert hall and the multifunctional hall. This back-to-back positioning makes it possible to share the central cloakroom and delivery facilities. The concert hall with seating for 1,200 also complies with top acoustic requirements. The diamond-shaped hall comprises curved stalls made of warm elm wood and wall and ceiling areas in pure white. Again, the sculptural, wave-shaped design of the components is important for the acoustics.

The façades of the performance areas also enclose the foyers, and the "cloud roof" is extended in lamella-shaped cantilevers so that the boundaries between inside and outside are blurred – the walk through the landscape of the Laoshan mountain range continues on the inside.

Visualisierung aus der Vorplanungsphase 2005
Visualization from the 2005 outline design phase

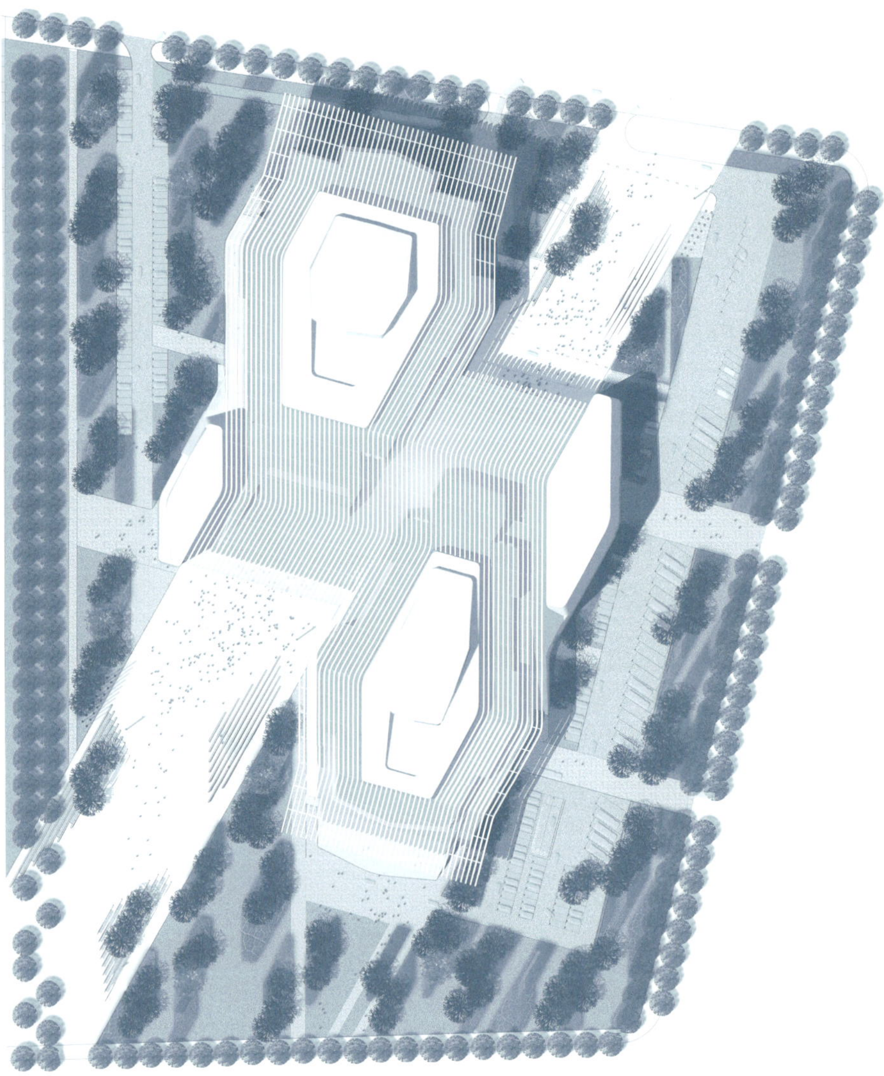

Lageplan
Site plan

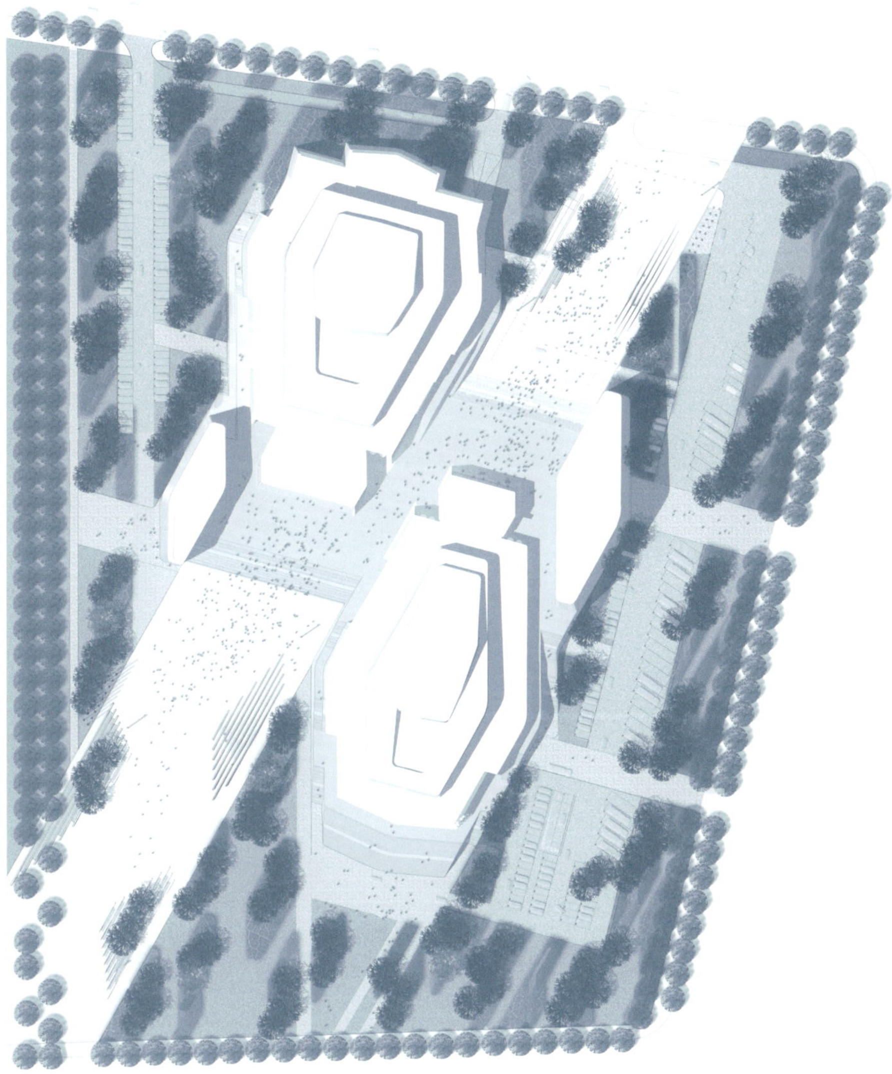

Lageplan ohne „Wolkendach“
Site plan without “cloud roof”

↗ Grundriss Funktionsgeschoss +-0,00m
Layout drawing of functional floor level +- 0.00

1	Opernbühne	Opera stage
2	Probesäle	Rehearsal rooms
3	Musikinstrumentenmuseum	Musical Instruments Museum
4	Restaurant	Restaurant
5	Bankettsaal	Banquet hall
6	Konferenzsäle	Conference halls
7	Hotellobby	Hotel lobby

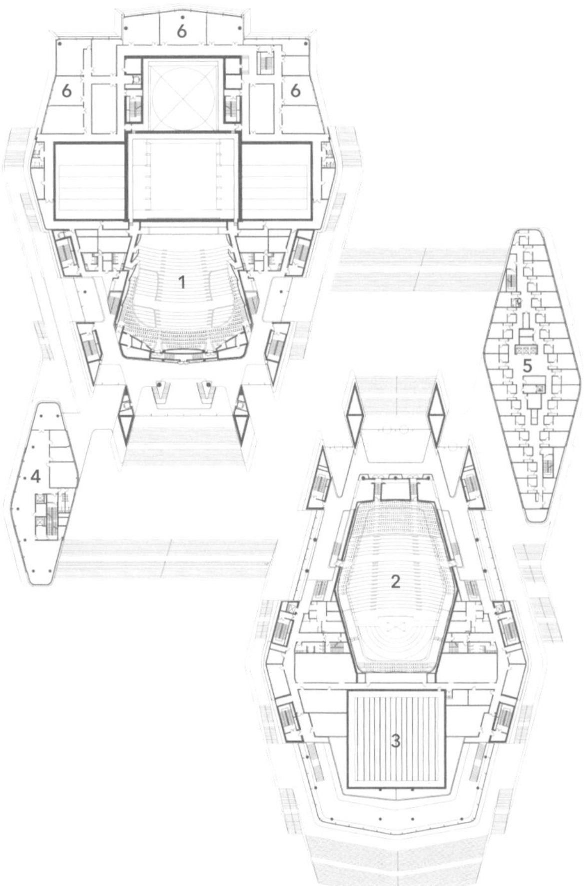

↗ Grundriss Saalgeschoss + 9,00 m
Layout drawing at auditorium level + 9.00 m

1	Opernsaal	Opera hall
2	Konzertsaal	Concert hall
3	Multifunktionshalle	Multifunctional hall
4	Musikinstrumentenmuseum	Musical instruments museum
5	Hotel	Hotel
6	Proberäume	Rehearsal rooms

Vogelperspektive mit Blick zum Gelben Meer
Bird's-eye view looking toward the Yellow Sea

Nördlicher Vorplatz mit Zugang zum Konzertsaal
Northern concourse with access to the concert hall

Das Grand Theater Qingdao - eine kulturgeschichtliche Einordnung

Eine Architekturkritik von Christian Brensing

Der Begriff der Oper, und demzufolge auch der eines Opernhauses, ist in China völlig anders besetzt als in Europa. Im Gegensatz zu der Europäischen Oper, wie sie sich über die Jahrhunderte in Italien, Frankreich oder Deutschland künstlerisch entwickelt hat, ist unter der Chinesischen Oper - einschließlich deren bekanntester Form, der sogenannten Peking-Oper - eine völlig anders geartete Kunstgattung zu verstehen. Zunächst einmal ist die Chinesische Oper wesentlich älter. Sie entstand während der Tang-Dynastie (618-906) aus Vorformen des Musiktheaters. Volksnah wurde sie mit wenigen Requisiten traditionell in Teehäusern aufgeführt. Legenden und Mythen aus der Volksgeschichte sind typische Themen, wobei eine ganze Palette von Ausdrucksformen zum Einsatz kommt: Musik, Gesang, Tanz, Schauspiel, Akrobatik oder gar Kampftechniken. Bis in das 20. Jahrhundert hinein wurden die Opern mündlich überliefert, erst dann mittels Partituren. Während der Kulturrevolution (1966-76) wurde die Chinesische Oper verboten, heute erfreut sie sich wieder einer größeren Beliebtheit und Verbreitung.

1

Gänzlich anders verlief die Entwicklung der Europäischen Oper mit Komponisten wie Rossini, Verdi, Puccini, Gounod, Wagner oder Richard Strauss. Einher mit der musikalischen Entwicklung der Oper geht bis zum heutigen Tag der Bau von repräsentativen Opernhäusern in den Metropolen der Welt. La Scala[1] in Mailand, La Fenice[2] in Venedig oder die Opernhäuser in Paris[3], Wien, Zürich und Dresden[4] sind die großen historischen Referenzbauten von legendärem Ruhm und weitreichender Ausstrahlung. Die Oper als Kunstform wurde im 19. Jahrhundert derart populär, dass man sie auch in aller Herren Länder „exportierte". Das exotischste dieser über die Welt verstreuten Opernhäuser ist wohl das legendäre Teatro Amazonas[5] (1896) in Manaus, Brasilien, welchem Werner Herzog in seinem Film „Fitzcarraldo" (1982) mit Klaus Kinski ein Denkmal setzte. Wo auch immer Opernhäuser gebaut wurden und werden, stehen sie stellvertretend für eine elitäre Hochkultur, die entsprechend gefördert und finanziert werden muss. Architektonisch sind Opernhäuser städtische Fixpunkte in den Stadtzentren, die großzügig und gut sichtbar über Plätze, Straßen, Alleen und mit Verkehrsmitteln aller Art ver- und angebunden sind. Oftmals finden sie sich in direkter Nachbarschaft zu Regierungsbauten, Museen, Kirchen und Theatern, was ihre hohe kulturelle Bedeutung noch weiter unterstreicht. In Europa kann man das Opernhaus als eine eigene, typologisch charakteristische Bauform bezeichnen.

Seit dem Aufsehen erregenden Neubau der Berliner Philharmonie[6] durch Hans Scharoun (1963) und dem Opernhaus[7] in Sydney des dänischen Architekten Jørn Utzon (1973) erlebte der Neubau von Opern- und Konzerthäusern, besonders in den letzten Jahrzehnten, weltweit eine gewisse Renaissance. Auf der Suche nach internationalem Prestige beauftragten Städte wie Luzern (Kultur- und Kongresszentrum, Jean Nouvel, 2003), Kopenhagen (Königliche Oper[8], Henning Larsen, 2005), Oslo (Neue Oper[9], Snøhetta, 2008) oder auch Hamburg (Elbphilharmonie[10], Herzog de Meuron, 2013) weltberühmte Architekten, die ihnen - gemessen an den Kriterien von Architektur, Ästhetik und Akustik - unvergleichliche Musiktempel entwarfen. Spektakulär müssen sie sein und das Stadtbild entsprechend prägen und formen, diese teuersten Kulturbauten aller Zeiten! Denn als Symbole und Ikonen eines neuen urbanen Selbstverständnisses buhlen sie neben Museen, Flughäfen oder Messehallen um internationale Aufmerksamkeit.

The Grand Theater Qingdao – a Cultural-historical Classification

An Architectural Criticism by Christian Brensing

The term "opera", and hence "opera house", carries completely different connotations in China from in Europe. In contrast to European opera, such as has developed artistically over the centuries in Italy, France, and Germany, Chinese opera – including its best-known form, Peking Opera – refers to a completely different genre of work.

To start with, Chinese opera goes back much further, to proto forms of musical theater in the Tang Dynasty (618–906). The popular form was traditionally performed in tea houses with few props. Typical subjects are legends and myths from folk history, whereby a whole range of expressive vehicles are used – music, song, dance, acting, acrobatics, or even combat. Until the 20th century, when scores were first used, operas were passed on orally. During the Cultural Revolution (1966–76), Chinese opera was forbidden. Today, it once again enjoys greater popularity and dissemination.

European opera developed quite differently in the hands of composers such as Rossini, Verdi, Puccini, Gounod, Wagner, and Richard Strauss. Even today, the musical development of opera goes hand in hand with the construction of prestigious opera houses in the major cities of the world. La Scala[1] in Milan, La Fenice[2] in Venice or the opera houses in Paris[3], Vienna, Zurich, and Dresden[4] are the great historical reference buildings of legendary fame and reputation. In the 19th century, opera became so popular as a form of art, that it was exported everywhere. The most exotic of these opera houses scattered all over the world is probably the legendary Teatro Amazonas[5] (1896) in Manaus/Brazil, which featured in Werner Herzog's film "Fitzcarraldo" (1982) with Klaus Kinski. Wherever opera houses were and are built, they represent an elite high culture that has to be promoted and financed accordingly. Architecturally, opera houses are fixed points on the urban scenes in city centers, grand, very visible buildings across squares, streets, and avenues and well positioned for public transport. Often, they are in the direct vicinity of government buildings, museums, churches, and theaters, which further underlines their high cultural value. In Europe, opera houses can be described as a typologically unique building form.

Even since the stir caused by Hans Scharoun's sensational new building for the Berlin Philharmonic[6] (1963), and Danish architect Jørn Utzon's Sydney Opera House[7] (1973), new opera houses and concert halls have enjoyed a worldwide renaissance, particularly in the last decades. In a quest for international prestige, cities such as Lucerne (Jean Nouvel's Culture and Congress Centre, 2003), Copenhagen (Royal Opera[8], Henning Larsen, 2005), Oslo (New Opera House[9], Snøhetta, 2008) and even Hamburg (Elbphilharmonie[10], Herzog/De Meuron, 2013) commissioned world-famous architects to design incomparable temples of music for them, as measured by the criteria of architecture, aesthetics, and acoustics. They had to be spectacular and leave their imprint on the urban scene, and form the most expensive cultural buildings of all time! As symbols and icons of a new urban self-image, they vie with museums, airports, and exhibition halls for international attention.

With the Chinese economic flowering of the last two decades, the desire for equally spectacular opera houses and concert halls also took hold in the cities of the Middle Kingdom. Resounding names of worldwide architectural prominence such as Paul Andreu, Zaha Hadid, Frederic Rolland, and von Gerkan, Marg and Partners (gmp) won international competitions with grandiose designs. gmp alone realized three combined opera houses and concert halls in China. Besides the "grand theater" in Qingdao, gmp completed two others in Chongqing and Tianjin by 2013. The term "grand theater" often conceals a multifunctional combination of at least two separate stages. In other words, in European tradition an opera house is combined with a concert hall into a single structure. For operators of grand theaters, that gener-

2

Mit der chinesischen Wirtschaftsblüte der letzten zwei Jahrzehnte etablierte sich auch der Wunsch, gleichermaßen spektakuläre Opern- und Konzerthäuser in den Metropolen des „Reichs der Mitte" zu errichten. Klingende Namen der weltweiten Architekturprominenz, wie Paul Andreu, Zaha Hadid, Frederic Rolland und auch von Gerkan, Marg und Partner (gmp), gewannen internationale Wettbewerbe mit grandiosen Entwürfen. gmp realisierten bis dato (Stand 2013) drei kombinierte Opern- und Konzerthäuser in China. Außer in Qingdao entstanden sogenannte „Grand Theater" auch in Chongqing und in Tianjin. Hinter dem Begriff „Grand Theater" verbirgt sich oftmals die multifunktionale Kombination von mindestens zwei eigenständigen Bühnen. Mit anderen Worten, in der europäischen Tradition wird ein Opernhaus mit einem Konzerthaus in einem einzigen Bauwerk integriert. Für den Betreiber des Grand Theater ergibt sich daraus eine logistische wie funktionale Synergie, die bei dem Management und der Vermarktung der Kultur klare Vorteile bringen. Ähnlich dem Prinzip von Sportarenen vereinen sich in einem Grand Theater nicht nur unterschiedliche Bühnen und entsprechende Kunstgattungen, sondern sie können zusätzlich noch zum Beispiel durch ein Museum, Einkaufspassagen, ein Hotel etc. ergänzt werden. Dem Einfallsreichtum der Bauherren oder Betreiber sind hier (fast) keine Grenzen gesetzt, sofern die jeweiligen „Bausteine" auf das engste aufeinander abgestimmt sind. Die Architektur hat dabei wahrlich Großartiges zu leisten, denn sie sollte aus der Nutzungsvielfalt ein architektonisch stimmiges Ensemble formen. Dies ist den Architekten von Gerkan, Marg und Partner (gmp) beim Qingdao Grand Theater in eindrucksvoller Weise gelungen.

3

Aus vielfältigen Ausdrucksformen eine formale Einheit zu schmieden, ist eines der architektonischen Leitmotive von gmp, unter das sie ihre architektonische Gestaltung seit vielen Jahrzehnten stellen. Statt einer abwechslungsreichen oder vielleicht auch nur beliebigen Architektursprache der mannigfaltigen Stile und Formen zu frönen, setzen gmp bewusst wenige, aber dafür umso stärkere Zeichen und Akzente. Musikalisch gesprochen, kann dies als Leitmotiv (wie zum Beispiel von dem deutschen Opernkomponisten Richard Wagner in seinen Werken praktiziert), also als das Aufgreifen eines Themas mit anschließenden Wiederholungen und Variationen, verstanden werden. Architektur ist dann in diesem Sinne „erstarrte Musik" (Schelling) oder „verstummte Tonkunst" (Goethe), deren dreidimensionaler Partitur das Auge und die Sinne folgen, bis hin zum vollständigen Verständnis des Bauwerks und seines Ortes. So erkennen die Besucher des Qingdao Grand Theater bestimmte Gesetzmäßigkeiten - ähnlich einem musikalischen Leitmotiv - die sich wiederholen, variiert werden, spiegeln oder gar negieren. Anhand der klar herausgearbeiteten baulichen Themen lässt sich die Architektur als eine Komposition entsprechend studieren und auch genießen.

Das am 28. Oktober 2010 offiziell eröffnete Qingdao Grand Theater liegt topografisch eingebettet zwischen dem pittoresken Laoshan-Gebirge und dem Gelben Meer in dem östlichsten Stadtteil der sich kilometerlang am Meer hinziehenden Stadt Qingdao. Thematisch nehmen die vier einzeln herausstehenden Baukörper, also 1. das Opernhaus (1600 Plätze), 2. das Konzerthaus (1200 Plätze) zusammen mit der Multifunktionshalle (400 Plätze), 3. das Musikinstrumentenmuseum und 4. das Hotel, mehr topografische als urbane Bezüge auf. Somit könnte man behaupten, dass das Grand Theater über seine städtische Umgebung hinaus erhaben ist.

4

5

ates both logistical and functional synergies that offer the management and marketing of culture clear benefits. Like the principle of sports arenas, a grand theater combines not only sundry stages and corresponding genres of art, but can also be supplemented with other items such as a museum, shopping mall, or hotel. There are (almost) no limits to the dreams of clients or operators here, provided the "components" concerned are closely attuned to each other. The architecture then really has its job cut out for it, since it has to make an architecturally coherent whole from the wide functional variety. That is just what architects von Gerkan, Marg and Partners (gmp) have pulled off most impressively at the Qingdao Grand Theater.

Forging formal unity from a variety of expressive forms is an architectural leitmotif at gmp, featuring in their architectural thinking for many decades. Instead of wallowing in variety or indulging in an idiom of "anything goes" in terms of style and form, gmp deliberately deploys just a few signs and accents, but uses them all the more powerfully. In a musical analogy, this might be understood in terms of a "leitmotif", as used by German opera composer Wagner in his works, whereby a particular theme is picked up with subsequent repetitions and variations. In this sense, architecture would be "petrified music" (in Schelling's term) or "silent music" (Goethe). Its three-dimensional score is followed by the eye and the senses until structure and its location have been completely absorbed. Thus, visitors to the Qingdao Grand Theater discern certain principles—akin to a musical leitmotif—that are repeated, varied, reflect each other, or even cancel each other out. Architecture can be understood and even enjoyed as a composition in terms of its clearly developed structural themes.

Officially opened on 28 October 2010, Qingdao Grand Theater is couched topographically between the picturesque Lao Shan Mountains and the Yellow Sea in the eastern part of the city of Qingdao, which extends for some miles along the seashore. Thematically, the four separate structures—1. the opera House (1,600 seats), 2. the concert hall (1,200 seats) with its multifunction hall (400 seats), 3. musical instruments museum and 4. hotel—respond more to topographical features than urban ones. One could say, for example, that the Grand Theater stands above its urban context. It stands out from the shimmering office towers of the business district and the mannered roof landscapes of the post-modernist residential blocks as a large white solid. Beyond all these constructional, stylistic flourishes, the Grand Theater intervenes symbolically between the forces of nature and symbolizes them—rocks and water. The rock surrounded (and thereby polished) by water is the thematic leitmotif of the architecture. The deliberate placing and positioning of the structure in the middle of a park stretching from the shore to the foot of the mountains picks up the theme and varies the process. The ground furrowed by water courses is the beginning of all landscapes, and in this way gains its characteristic appearance. The architects could have scarcely made the references to the place more relevant or distinctive. The Grand Theater is thus hallmarked with an immediately recognizable absence of ambivalence. The strength and power of the design resides in the recognizability associated therewith.

The variations of the leitmotif are asserted architecturally in a number of ways. Individual parts of the building, perspectives, glimpses of the interior, and outward views and the materiality all play an outstanding role.

6

7

Als großes weißes Massiv hebt es sich von den schillernden Bürotürmen des Business District und den manierierten Dachlandschaften der postmodernen Wohnblöcke ab. Jenseits all dieser baulich-stilistischen Schnörkel vermittelt das Grand Theater stattdessen symbolisch zwischen den Naturgewalten und stellt diese stellvertretend dar: Felsen und Wasser. Der vom Wasser umströmte und dadurch geschliffene Stein ist das thematische Leitmotiv der Architektur. Die bewusste Setzung und Positionierung der Baukörper inmitten eines Parks, der sich vom Strand bis zum Fuße des Gebirges erstreckt, nimmt das Thema auf und variiert diesen Prozess. Denn die von Wasserläufen zerfurchte Erde ist der Beginn einer jeden Landschaft; sie erhält auf diese Weise ihr erstes charakteristisches Aussehen. Markanter und ortsrelevanter hätten die Architekten die Bezüge kaum aufnehmen können. Und so ist das Grand Theater zeichenhaft mit einer sofort erkennbaren Eindeutigkeit belegt. In dieser damit verbundenen Wiedererkennbarkeit liegt die Stärke und Größe des Entwurfs.

Die Variationen des Leitmotivs kommen architektonisch mehrschichtig zur Geltung. Einzelne Gebäudeteile, Perspektiven, Ein- wie Ausblicke und die Materialität spielen dabei eine herausragende Rolle, so die projektverantwortlichen Architekten. „Es gibt eine klare symbolische Entsprechung von Wolken und Bergmassiv, gleichzeitig haben wir aber versucht, dieses landschaftliche Thema auch räumlich umzusetzen. Die Dynamik der Lineaturen, ablesbar an den horizontalen Fassadenlinien und den Dachlamellen, ziehen einen in die Tiefe des Raums. Diese landschaftlich frei interpretierte Form basiert allerdings auf einer eindeutigen geometrischen Struktur, nämlich einem vertikalen Gebäuderaster von 45 Zentimetern, welches horizontal sämtliche Baukörper definiert und verbindet. Nur an diesen Sedimentlinien scheren die Baukörper ab bzw. verbinden sich an einer anderen Stelle wieder. Selbst die Treppenstufen, jeweils drei à 15 Zentimeter Höhe, ordnen sich in diese Struktur ein. Weiterhin haben wir neben dem rechten Winkel nur noch einen 15-Grad-Winkel in der Grundrissstruktur des Gebäudes, sämtliche Schrägen unterliegen dieser Ordnung. Buchstäblich kontrollieren die „Sedimentscheiben" die strukturelle Einheit des Bauwerks."

Das Ensemble der Bauten ist durch eine offene, linear geschwungene Lamellendachstruktur miteinander verwoben und geleitet die Besucher über weit ausladende Freitreppen auf eine 4,50 Meter hoch liegende Terrasse, von der aus man in alle Bereiche gelangt. Übertragen strömen die Menschen entweder vom Meer her oder vom Gebirge kommend zum und durch das Grand Theater und ihr Blick geht zwangsläufig von der Terrasse hinüber auf die eine oder andere natürliche Kulisse. Optisch lässt man die Stadt hinter sich und wendet sich im Blick zunächst der grandiosen Natur und erst dann der Kunst und Kultur zu. Die Wege zur Kunst sind somit durch die Architektur vorgegeben. Sie leben vom Ort und lassen uns ihn erleben. Dabei durchlaufen die Besucher einen bewussten Prozess. Die Linearität der nach Oben hin konisch zulaufenden und mit weißem Shandong-Bei-Ma-Granit verkleideten Baukörper spielt darin eine ebenso große Rolle wie auch der parallele Schwung der bis zu sechs Meter tiefen und teilweise über 100 Meter langen Dachelemente. Letztere spenden Schatten, aber der eigentliche Sinn und Zweck der Lamellen ist die große, raumgreifende Wirkung. Sie verbindet das Opern- und Konzerthaus wie auch das Museum und das Hotel auf das engste, vielleicht auch im übertragenen Sinne das Gelbe Meer mit dem Laoshan-Gebirge! Die Leichtigkeit der Linienführung kontrastiert die Masse und Geschlossenheit der Fassaden, die nur an wenigen bestimmten Punkten von großen Glasfassaden oder vielen langen und schmalen, übereinander gesetzten

8

Fensterschlitzen durchbrochen werden. Wie horizontal geschichtete Sedimente liegen die Fassadenlinien aufeinander und leiten die Blicke entlang der weich abgeschliffenen Baukörper. Keine spitzen Winkel oder Ecken stören die Harmonie dieses in sich ruhenden Bauwerks. Und dennoch strahlt es eine gehörige Portion von Dynamik und Eleganz aus, wie die Architekten erläutern:

9

The responsible architects: "There is a clear symbolic correspondence between the waves of water and the mountain massif, but at the same time, we tried to implement this landscape theme spatially as well. The dynamic of line, readable in the horizontal façade lines and roof lamellae, draws you into the depth of the space. Admittedly, this freely interpreted landscape form is based on an unambiguous geometrical structure, i.e., a vertical building grid of forty-five-centimeters, which defines and connects all the buildings horizontally. The structures sheer off or connect up again elsewhere only at these sediment lines. Even the steps, each three of them fifteen centimeters high, fit into this structure. In addition, we have apart from right angles only a 15° angle in the ground plan structure of the building, and all diagonals are subject to this system. The 'sediment plates' literally control the structural unity of the building."

The buildings are interwoven into an ensemble by an open, curved linear lamella roof structure. Visitors are guided across broad open-air steps to a 4.5-meter-high terrace, from which all areas can be accessed. Figuratively, people come either from the sea or the mountains to and through the Grand Theater, and their eyes pass out of necessity across the terrace toward one or the other natural backdrop. Visually, you leave the city behind you, and turn to look at the grandeur of nature, and only then at art and culture. Access to art is thus specified by the architecture. The routes are part of the place, and help us to experience it. Visitors are thus subject to a conscious process. The linearity of the structures, which taper conically upwards and are clad with white Shandong Bei Ma granite, is as much a part of that as the parallel curve of the roof elements, which are up to six meters deep and in some cases over one hundred meters long. The latter cast shadows, but the ultimate purpose of the lamellae is the key spatial effect. They closely connect the opera house and concert hall with the museum and hotel, and perhaps also in figurative sense, the Yellow Sea with the Laoshan mountains. The lightness of the linearity offsets the mass and unity of the façades, which are interrupted by glass façades only in few places here and there, or numerous long, narrow window slits on top of each other. The lines of the façades run like horizontally layered sediments, and guide the eye along the softly polished building. No sharp angles or corners disrupt the harmony of this well-balanced structure. And even so, it exudes a due portion of dynamism and elegance, as the architects explains:

"Because of the controlled geometry, I can follow a line—which, for example, existed previously as a terrace level—in the building at any time. It is the horizontal lines that constantly pull the whole ensemble together. The structurally very strong foundation—which gmp, in comparison with many others of its buildings, interprets very freely—is the basis of the design. It only needs a few details to get the whole building. The result of that is a definability and constructability, but ultimately is what accounts for the classic elegance of the Qingdao Grand Theater."

After the external flights of steps, visitors enter the multistory foyers of the opera house and concert hall and multifunctional hall. The latter is admittedly designed purely functionally as a black box. On the other hand, the auditoria of the opera house and concert hall are designed as showpieces. The dazzling white of the horizontally arranged façade structure is followed in the auditorium of the opera house by alternating vertical red and black concrete elements in glass-fiber reinforced concrete (GRC). The heavy, ten-centimeter elements are grooved to different depths according to frequency bands, and guarantee excellent acoustics. The visual impression is reminiscent of the festive atmosphere of European opera houses. The concert hall, with its elm veneer, is in contrast much lighter. The horizontal white wall-cladding above bows out three-dimensionally, and this is accentuated by appropriate lighting. Here too the fluid, undulating line is continued formally. Many of these sighting alignments run in both auditoria toward the stage.

10

„Auf Grund der kontrollierten Geometrie kann man jederzeit eine Linie – die zum Beispiel vorher als Terrassenebene existiert – in dem Gebäude weiterverfolgen. Es sind die horizontalen Linien, die das gesamte Bauwerk immer wieder zusammenziehen. Diese strukturelle sehr starke Grundlage, die gmp – im Vergleich zu vielen anderen ihrer Bauten – sehr frei interpretieren, ist die Basis des Entwurfs. Mit wenigen Details kann man das ganze Haus bespielen. Daraus leitet sich eine Definierbarkeit, Baubarkeit, aber letztendlich auch die klassische Eleganz des Qingdao Grand Theater ab."

Nach den äußeren Treppenkaskaden betritt der Besucher die mehrgeschossigen Foyers von Opern- und Konzerthaus wie auch der Multifunktionshalle. Letztere ist allerdings nur rein funktional als Black Box ausgebaut. Dagegen sind die Säle von Opern- und Konzerthaus repräsentativ gestaltet. Dem blendenden Weiß der horizontal angelegten Fassadenstruktur folgen im Auditorium des Opernhauses vertikale, abwechselnd in rotschwarz gehaltene glasfaserverstärkte Betonelemente (GRC). Circa zehn Zentimeter stark, schwer in der Masse und gemäß den Frequenzbereichen mit unterschiedlich tiefen Kanneluren durchzogen, garantieren sie eine hervorragende Raumakustik. Der visuelle Raumeindruck erinnert an die festliche Stimmung europäischer Opernhäuser. Im Unterschied dazu ist der Konzertsaal mit seinem Furnier aus Ulmenholz farblich viel heller gehalten. Die darüber horizontal verlaufende weiße Wandverkleidung schwingt dreidimensional vor und zurück, was durch eine entsprechende Beleuchtung noch zusätzlich akzentuiert wird. Auch hier setzt sich formal eine fließende und wellenförmige Linienfügung fort. Viele dieser linearen Sichtbezüge laufen in beiden Sälen auf die Bühne zu.

Weitaus bedeutender als die Optik ist jedoch die Akustik in Opern- und Konzertauditorien. In der Tradition des europäischen Musiktheaters gibt es bestimmte Meilensteine, wie zum Beispiel Wagners Festspielhaus in Bayreuth oder Scharouns Berliner Philharmonie[11], die sich durch eine besondere Akustik im direkten Verbund mit der Gestaltung des Auditoriums auszeichnen. Architektur und Musik gehen hier eine einzigartige Verbindung von Form und akustischer Funktion ein. Ein Zustand, der heute leider immer seltener wird, da die Bühnen nicht mehr als Aufführungsorte einer einzigen Kunstgattung dienen. Die Kulturindustrie von heute bedarf flexibler und höchst unterschiedlicher technischer und funktionaler Bedingungen. So sind auch die Bühnen des Qingdao Grand Theater gleichzeitig für höchst unterschiedliche Kunstformen ausgelegt. Rein technisch betrachtet kann dort alles auf der Bühne aufgeführt werden, von der aufführungstechnisch äußerst anspruchsvollen europäischen Oper bis hin zu Musicals, Tanz- oder Fernsehshows. Bei beiden Sälen stand jedoch immer die rein raumakustische, das heißt unverstärkte Aufführung als Planungsaufgabe im Vordergrund. Diese Vielfalt müssen heutige Bühnen bieten, damit sie im internationalen Wettbewerb um Künstler und Produktionen bestehen können. Das Qingdao Grand Theater wird in dieser Hinsicht allen Erwartungen der Künstler, Produzenten und Zuschauer gerecht. Im Einklang mit seiner bemerkenswerten architektonischen Sprache und seiner multifunktionalen Nutzbarkeit ist es zu einem der modernsten und anspruchsvollsten Grand Theaters in China geworden. Sprichwörtlich ein Gesamtkunstwerk wo gemäß der chinesischen ebenso wie der europäischen Tradition Opern und Musikstücke aufgeführt werden können.

However, acoustics are much more important than looks in opera houses and concert halls. In the tradition of the European musical theater, there are certain milestones such as Wagner's Festspielhaus in Bayreuth or Scharoun's Berlin Philharmonic, which stand out for special acoustics directly associated with the design of the auditorium. Architecture and music fuse here in a unique combination of form and acoustic function—a state that is unfortunately ever rarer these days, as stages are no longer used for performances of a single artistic genre. Today's culture industry needs flexible and highly differentiated technical and functional backup. The stages of the Qingdao Grand Theater are therefore set up simultaneously for highly different forms of art. From a purely technical point of view, everything can be performed on the stage there, from the most technically demanding European opera to musicals, dance shows, and TV shows. In both auditoria, however, the purely acoustic dimension—i.e., unreinforced performance—was the prime design consideration. Modern stages have to provide this variety in order keep up with the competition for artistes and productions.

11

In this respect, the Qingdao Grand Theater will meet the expectations of all artists, producers, and audiences. In harmony with its remarkable architectural idiom and multifunctional practicality, it is one of the most modern and ambitious grand theaters in China—a work of total art where operas and music can be performed in accordance with both Chinese and European tradition.

Fotografische Dokumentation

Photographic Documentation

← Blick auf den Künstlereingang und das Instrumentenmuseum. Die Linearität der nach oben konisch zulaufenden und mit weißem Granit verkleideten Baukörper wird durch die schmalen Fensterbänder betont.
View of the artists' entrance and the Instrument Museum. The lines of the white granite cladding, which conically reduce towards the top, are emphasized by the narrow fenestration bands.

↑ Blick von Südosten
View from the southeast

← Blick auf den Haupteingang der Oper. Die bis zu sechs Meter tiefen und teilweise über 100 Meter langen Dachelemente erzeugen eine raumgreifende Wirkung.
View of the main entrance to the Opera House. The roof elements, which are up to 6 meter deep and over 100 meter long create a key spatial effect.

↑ Nördliche Freitreppe mit Blick auf den Bühnenturm der Oper
The northern open-air steps with view of the stage tower of the Opera House

← ◫ Pausenterrasse des Konzertsaals mit Blick zum Meer
The concert hall's interval terrace with a view to the ocean

Das Ensemble der Bauten ist durch eine offene, linear geschwungene Lamellendachstruktur miteinander verwoben und geleitet die Besucher über weit ausladende Freitreppen auf eine Terrasse, von der man in alle Bereiche gelangt.
The buildings are interwoven into an ensemble by an open, curved linear lamella roof structure. Visitors are guided across broad open-air steps to a terrace, from which all areas can be accessed.

↑ Das harmonische Zusammenspiel aller Baukörper wird durch die parallel schwingenden Dachlamellen, die waagerecht geprägte Linienführung der geschlossenen Fassaden im Außen- und Innenraum, die schmalen eingeschnittenen Fensterbänder und die Gliederung der Glasfassaden betont.
The harmonious interplay of all building elements is emphasized by the sweeping parallel roof elements, the predominantly horizontal lines of the enclosing façades of the exterior and interior, the narrow recessed fenestration bands and the design of the glass façades.

→ Foyer des Multifunktionssaals mit Aufgang zur Empore
Foyer of the multifunctional hall with access to the balcony

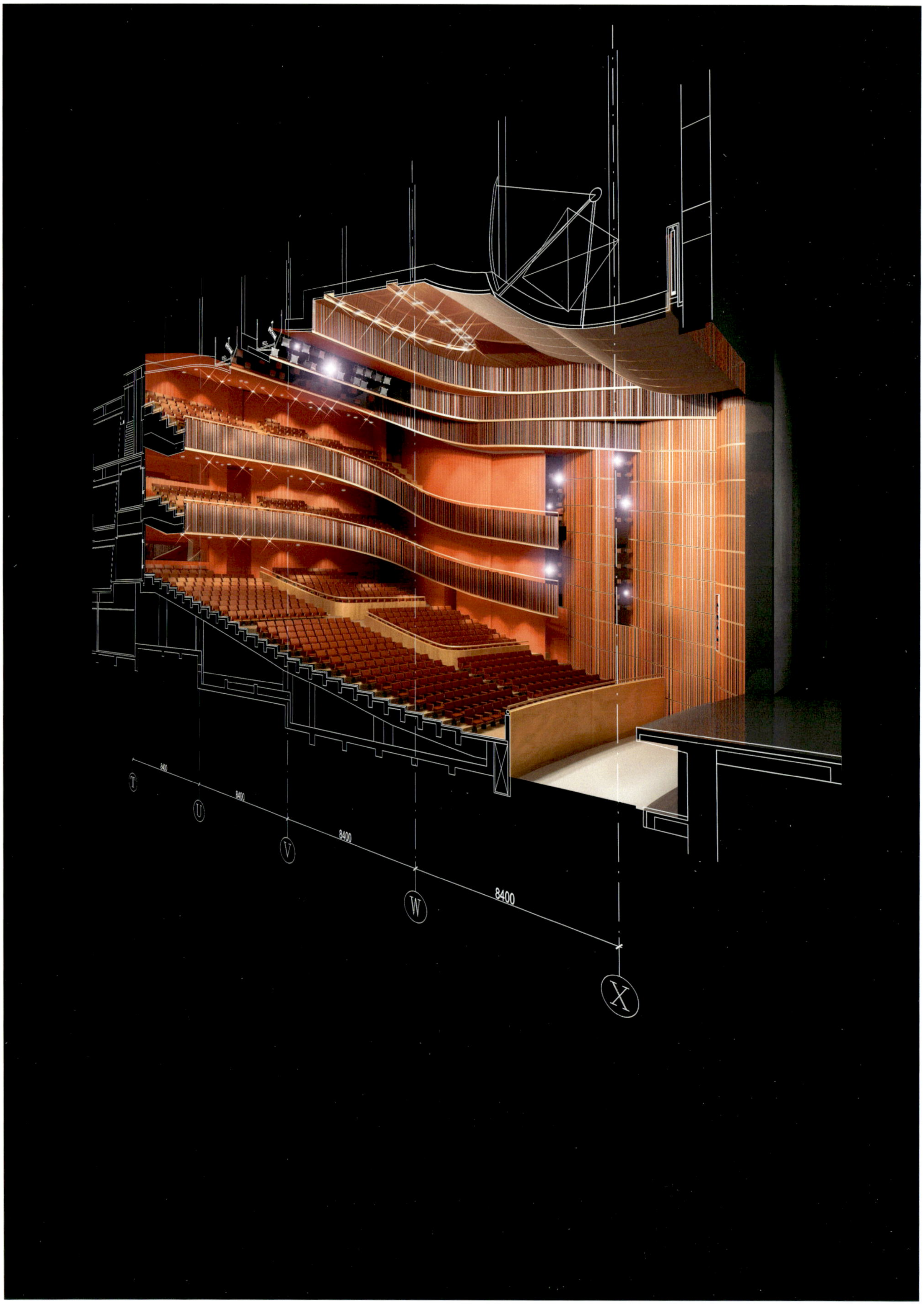
8400
8400
8400
8400
T
U
V
W
X

← ◫ Foyer des Opernhauses, das wie der Saal mit plastischen Betonpaneelen verkleidet ist.
Foyer of the Opera House, which—like the auditorium—is lined with sculptural concrete panels.

← Schnittperspektive des Opernsaals
Sectional perspective of the Opera House auditorium

↑ Der Opernsaal bietet Platz für 1600 Zuschauer.
The Opera House auditorium has 1,600 seats.

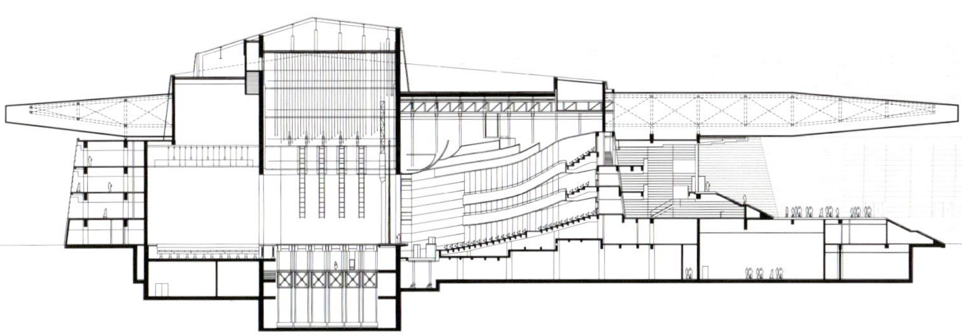

← Die differenzierte Ausbildung der plastischen Betonpaneele erzeugt eine Raumakustik auf internationalem Niveau.
The sophisticated design of the sculptural concrete panels generates acoustic conditions meeting international standards.

↑ Der Saal orientiert sich an klassischen europäischen Opernhäusern. Zahlreiche Ränge umgeben das Parkett hufeisenförmig.
The auditorium is designed along classic European lines. The stalls are surrounded by numerous balconies in the shape of a horseshoe.

↑ Längsschnitt Opernhaus
Longitudinal section through the Opera House

↖ Der Raumeindruck erinnert an die Festlichkeit europäischer Opernhäuser.
The visual impression is reminiscent of the festive character of European opera houses.

↑ Im Kontrast zum Opernsaal verleihen die weiße Decke und das Ulmenholzfurnier des Parketts dem Konzertsaal seinen heiteren Charakter.
In contrast to the Opera House auditorium, the white ceiling and elm wood veneer of the concert hall stalls impart a cheerful character.

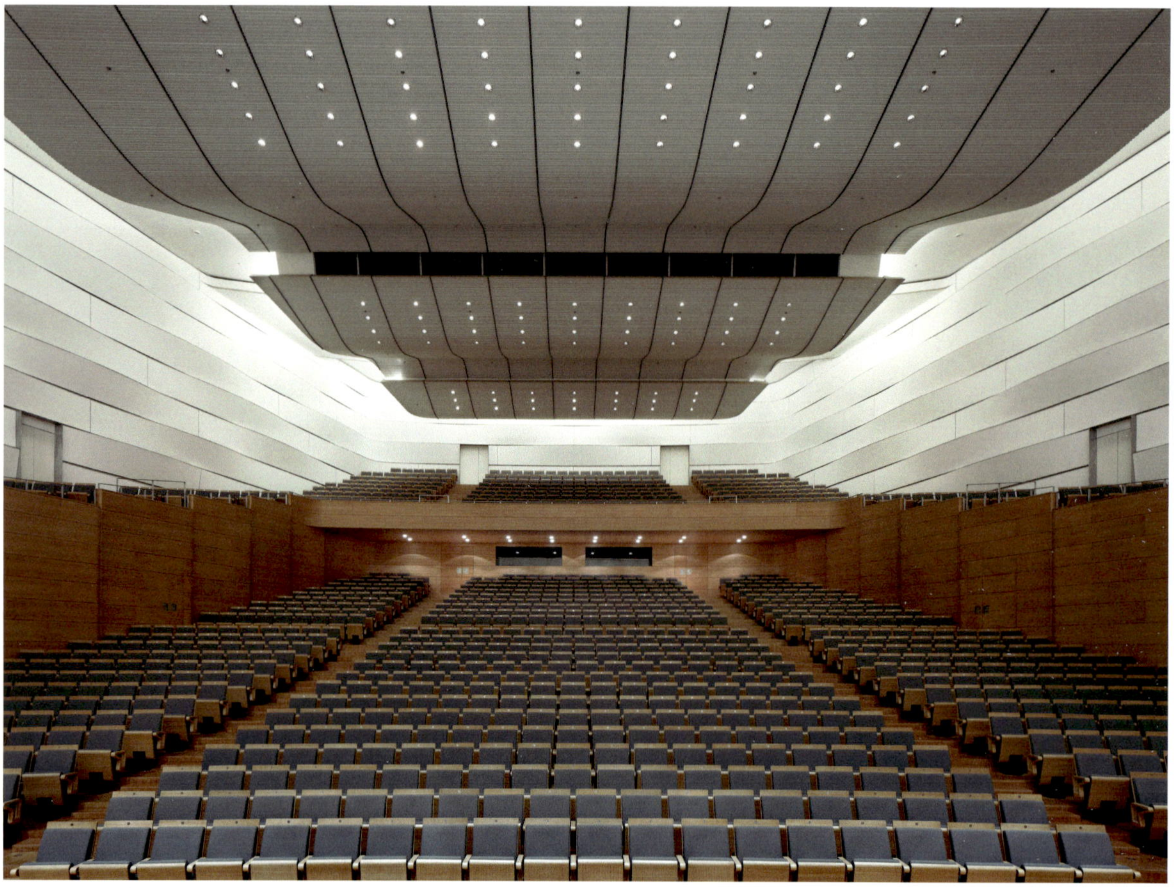

↑ Der rombenförmig geschnittene Saal bietet Platz für 1200 Personen.
The layout of the auditorium is diamond-shaped and has seating for 1,200.

↗ Die weiße Wandverkleidung aus Gipskarton schwingt dreidimensional vor und zurück und unterstützt damit die hohe akustische Qualität des Konzertsaals.
The white plasterboard lining of the walls recedes and protrudes to produce a three-dimensional effect and enhances the high quality of the concert hall acoustics.

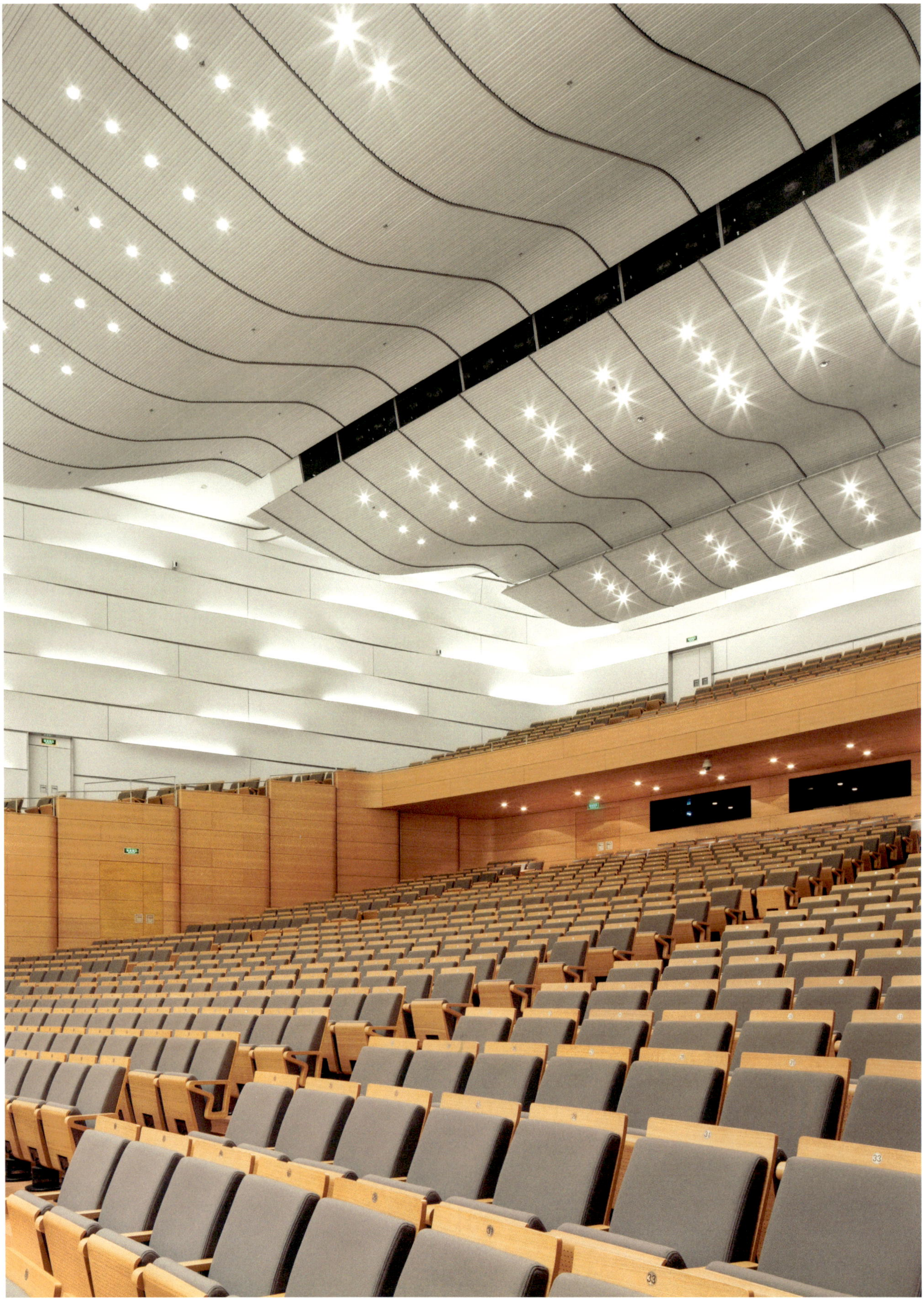

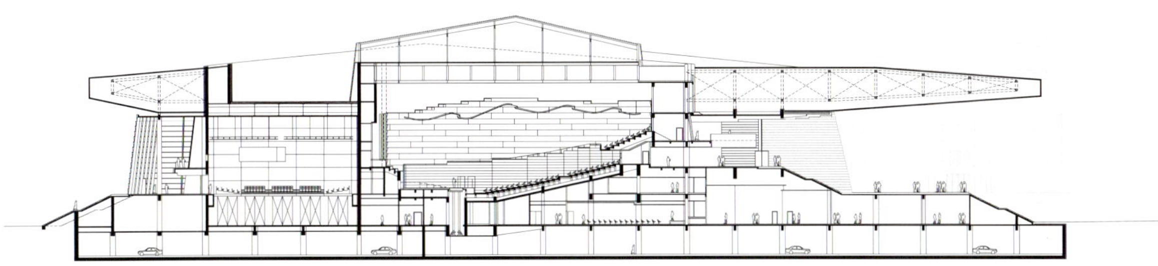

← Der Einsatz von Licht akzentuiert die Bauteile.
The lighting has been arranged to accentuate the building components.

↑ Die plastische wellenförmige Ausbildung der Bauteile trägt zur ausgezeichneten Akustik bei und symbolisiert das Meer Qingdaos.
The sculptural, wavy design of the building elements contributes to the excellent acoustics, while also symbolizing the ocean surrounding Qingdao.

↑ Längsschnitt Konzerthalle
Longitudinal section of the concert hall

↑ Sämtliche Bauteile sind plastisch geformt, um eine ausgewogene Raumakustik zu erzeugen.
All building components have a sculptured design in order to generate a balanced acoustic effect.

→ Schnittperspektive Konzertsaal
Sectional perspective of the concert hall

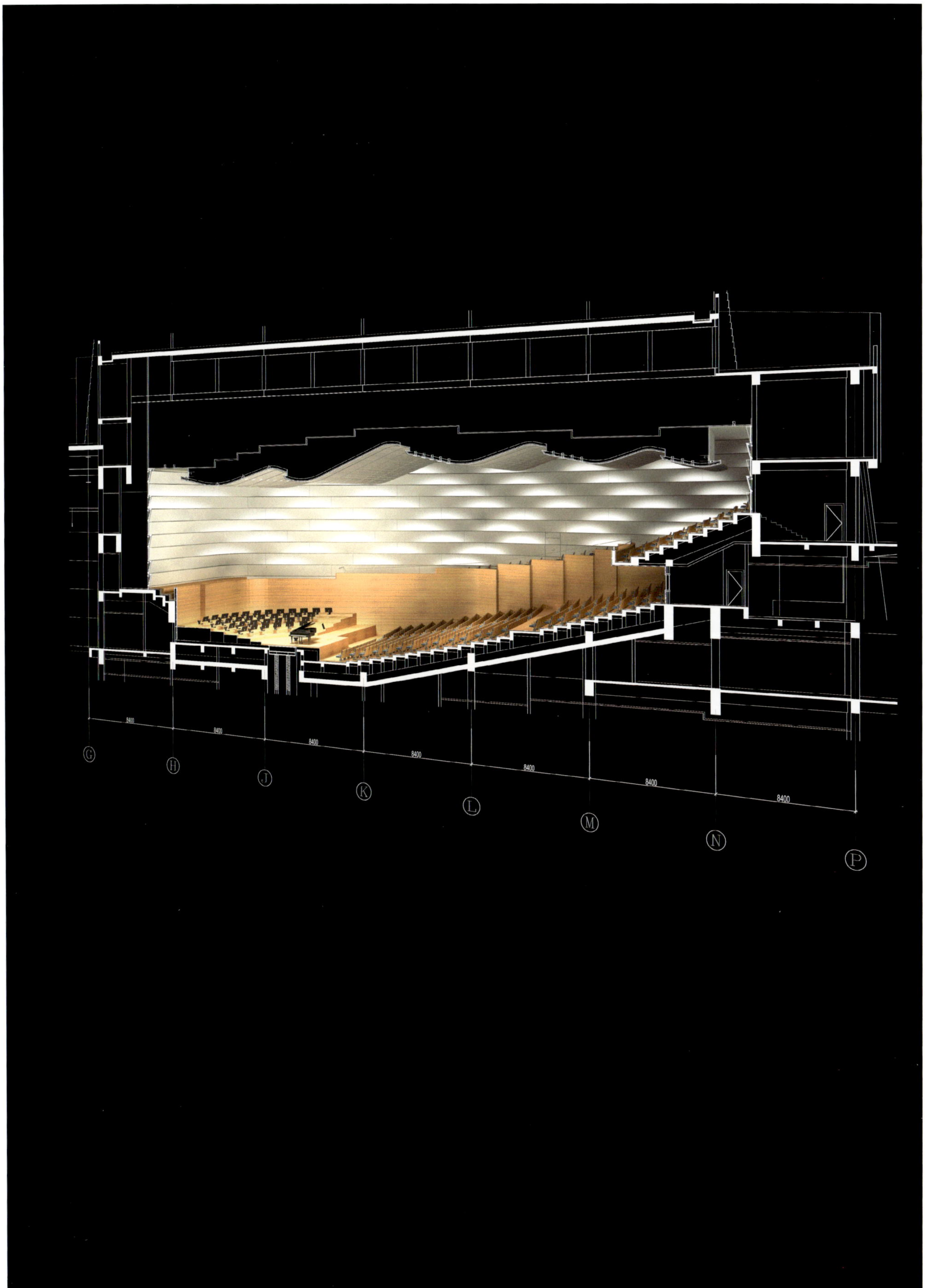
8400
8400
8400
8400
8400
8400
8400
G
H
J
K
L
M
N
P

↑ Eine mobile Bestuhlung erlaubt bis zu 400 Sitzplätze.
There is mobile seating for up to 400 visitors.

↑ Die als „Black Box" ausgebildete Multifunktionshalle bietet Raum für unterschiedlichste Nutzungen.
The multifunctional hall has been designed as a "black box" and can accommodate a wide range of functions.

Auch im mehrgeschossigen Foyer sind der parallele Schwung der Dachelemente und die horizontale Gliederung des hellen Granits für die Besucher erlebbar.
The parallel curves of the roof elements and the horizontal structure of the light granite can also be experienced by visitors in the multistory foyer.

Blick in das Opernfoyer entlang der Passage, die den nördlichen mit dem südlichen Vorplatz verbindet
View into the foyer of the Opera House along the passage linking the northern and southern concourses

Haupteingang des Opernhauses
mit festlicher Beleuchtung
Main entrance to the Opera House
with festive lighting

Illuminierte Ansicht des südlichen Vorplatzes
View of the illuminated southern concourse

Anhang

Appendix

Entwurfsteam Design team

gmp

Meinhard von Gerkan

Prof. Dr. h. c. mult. Dipl.-Ing. Architekt BDA

Gründungspartner, geboren 1935 in Riga/Lettland, 1965 Gründungspartner des Architekturbüros von Gerkan, Marg und Partner zusammen mit Volkwin Marg, 1974 Berufung an die TU Carolo-Wilhelmina zu Braunschweig als ordentlicher Professor/Lehrstuhl A für Entwerfen und Institutsleiter des Instituts für Baugestaltung A, Mitglied Freie Akademie der Künste zu Hamburg, 2005 Verleihung der Ehrendoktorwürde für Entwerfen durch die Chung Yuan Christian University in Chung Li/Taiwan, 2007 Verleihung der Ehrenprofessur durch das East China Normal University College of Design, Shanghai/China, 2007 Präsident der Academy for Architectural Culture (aac), zahlreiche Auszeichnungen, u. a. Fritz Schumacher Preis, Rumänischer Staatspreis, Plakette der Freien Akademie der Künste Hamburg, Großer Preis des Bundes Deutscher Architekten, Verleihung des Bundesverdienstkreuzes.

Founding partner, born 1935 in Riga/Latvia; 1965 co-founder with Volkwin Marg of the architectural partnership of von Gerkan, Marg and Partners; 1974 appointed professor, chair A for Design at the Carolo-Wilhelmina Technical University in Brunswick, head of Institute A for Architectural Design, member of the Freie Akademie der Künste in Hamburg; 2005 honorary doctorate in design from Chung Yuan Christian University in Chung Li/Taiwan; 2007 honorary professor, East China Normal University College of Design, Shanghai/China; 2007 president of the Academy for Architectural Culture (aac). Numerous awards, including Fritz Schumacher Prize, Romanian State Prize, bronze plaque of the Freie Akademie der Künste, Hamburg, BDA Prize, Federal Cross of Merit.

Stephan Schütz

Dipl.-Ing. Architekt BDA

Partner, geb. 1966 in Duisburg, seit 2006 Partner im Büro von Gerkan, Marg und Partner, Leitung der gmp-Büros Berlin, Peking, Shenzhen, Projekte u.a. Weimarhalle, Tempodrom, Berlin, Christliche Kirche, Peking, CYTS Plaza, Peking, Opernhaus Qingdao, Chinesisches Nationalmuseum, Peking, Sportzentrum Shenzhen.

Partner, born 1966 in Duisburg, graduate architect; partner at von Gerkan, Marg and Partners since 2006; management of the gmp offices in Berlin, Beijing and Shenzhen; projects include New Weimar Hall, New Tempodrom, Berlin, Christian Church, Beijing, CYTS Plaza, Beijing, Qingdao Grand Theater, National Museum of China, Beijing, Shenzhen Universiade Sports Center.

gmp

Nicolas Pomränke
Dipl.-Ing. Architekt

Assoziierter Partner, geb. 1970 in Wuppertal, seit 2010 assoziierter Partner im Büro von Gerkan, Marg und Partner, Projektleitungen u. a. Zhongguancun Cultural Center, Grand Theater, Qingdao, Kulturpalast Dresden.

Associate partner, born Wuppertal 1970; associate partner at von Gerkan, Marg and Partners since 2010; project management of Zhongguancun Cultural Center, Grand Theater/Qingdao, Kulturpalast/Dresden, among others.

Clemens Kampermann
Dipl.-Ing. Architekt

Assoziierter Direktor, geb. 1977 in Celle/Deutschland, seit 2012 assoziierter Direktor im Büro von Gerkan, Marg und Partner, Mitarbeit u.a. Grand Theater, Qingdao; Projektleitungen u. a. Qingdao International Finance Plaza; Zhuhai Museum; Hengqin Headquarters, Zhuhai.

Associate Director, born 1977 in Celle/Germany; since 2012 associate director at von Gerkan, Marg and Partners; team member for Grand Theater, Qingdao, among others; project management of: Qingdao International Finance Plaza, Zhuhai Museum, Hengqin Headquarters, Zhuhai, among others.

gmp Partner China

Wu Wei
Dipl. Architekt ETH

Partner für China – geboren 1971 in Lanzhou/Gansu, China, 1992 Abschluss des Architektustudiums in Chongqing, China, 1992–94 Architekt am Gansu Institute of Architectural Design, 1994–95 Studium der Deutschen Sprache in der Schweiz, 1995–97 Architekturstudium ETH Zürich und 1997–2000 Mitarbeit im Büro Skyline Architecture und in der Firma SwissGerman Consulting in Zürich, 2000 Diplom an der ETH Zürich am Lehrstuhl Prof. Mario Campi, seit 2000 Mitarbeit im Büro von Gerkan, Marg und Partner Architekten, seit 2001 Chefrepräsentant der gmp-Büros in Peking und Shanghai, seit 2004 assoziierter Partner im Büro von Gerkan, Marg und Partner, seit 2009 Partner für China im Büro von Gerkan, Marg und Partner.

Partner for China, born 1971 in Lanzhou/Gansu, China; completed architectural studies in Chongqing, China, in 1992. From 1992 to 1994 architect at the Gansu Institute of Architectural Design, 1994 to 1995 German language studies in Switzerland, 1995 to 1997 studied architecture at the ETH Zurich and from 1997 to 2000 worked for Skyline Architecture and SwissGerman Consulting in Zurich; qualified at ETH Zurich (Prof. Mario Campi) in 2000, since then work for von Gerkan, Marg and Partners, Architects (gmp); since 2001 chief representative of gmp's offices in Beijing and Shanghai, since 2004 Associate Partner with von Gerkan, Marg and Partners and since 2009 Partner at gmp with responsibility for China.

Autor Author

Christian Brensing
M.A. (RCA) / Autor und Journalist Author and Journalist

Geboren 1960 in Bad Ems, 1982–89 Studium der englischen Literatur und Kunstgeschichte, Abschluss M.A. Royal College of Art (RCA), London; 1989–90 wissenschaftlicher Assistent am Royal College of Art, London; 1990–92 Zaha Hadid Architects in London; 1993–2004 Ove Arup & Partners Consulting Engineers, London und Berlin; 2004–05 CBP Consulting Engineers, München; seit 2006 freischaffender Berater, Autor und Kurator; 2012 Gründung Christian Brensing Enterprises Ltd. London/Berlin.

Born 1960 in Bad Ems, studied English Literature and History of Art from 1982–89, final degree M.A. Royal College of Art (RCA), London; 1989–90 assistant lecturer, Royal College of Art, London; 1990–92 Zaha Hadid Architects, London; 1993–2004 Ove Arup & Partners Consulting Engineers, London and Berlin; 2004–05 CBP Consulting Engineers, Munich; since 2006 freelance consultant, author and curator; 2012 founded Christian Brensing Enterprises Ltd., London/Berlin.

Fotografen Photographers

Christian Gahl

Geboren 1966 in München, 1993-96 Studium der Architektur, seit 1996 selbstständiger Architekturfotograf, international tätig u.a. für Architekturbüros Hild + K., Toyo Ito, Murphy/Jahn, Rem Koolhaas, HG Merz, Künstler wie Keith Sonnier, Ulrich Rückriem, Walter de Maria, Institutionen wie das Guggenheim New York, MoMA New York und die Neue Nationalgalerie Berlin, publiziert u.a. in „The Architectural Review"„ „A+U", „domus", „Neue Zürcher Zeitung".

Born 1966 in Munich, studied architecture from 1993-96, since 1996 freelance architectural photographer with international commissions for architects Hild + K., Toyo Ito, Murphy/Jahn, Rem Koolhaas and HG Merz, artists such as Keith Sonnier, Ulrich Rückriem, Walter de Maria and institutions such as the Guggenheim New York, the MoMA New York and the new National Gallery in Berlin, published in "The Architectural Review", "A+U", "domus" and "Neue Zürcher Zeitung"

Hans-Georg Esch

geboren 1964 in Neuwied, klassische Fotoausbildung, seit 1989 freischaffender Architekturfotograf, zählt heute zu den renommiertesten Vertretern seines Fachs, neben Auftragsarbeiten eigenständiges Œuvre freier künstlerischer Arbeit, bekannt durch international ausgestellte und publizierte Fotostrecken: „Megacities", „City and Structure", „Cities Unknown", Esch lebt und arbeitet in Hennef/ Stadt Blankenberg.

Born 1964 in Neuwied; classic photography training; since 1989, freelance architectural photographer; today he is one of the best known proponents of his subject; in addition to contract work, he produces his own independent artistic oeuvre; he is well known through internationally exhibited and published photo series: "Megacities", "City and Structure", "Cities Unknown"; Esch lives and works in Hennef, Stadt Blankenberg.

Projektdaten Project Data

Bauherr Client
Qingdao Conson Industrial Corporation

Intern. Wettbewerb Int'l. competition
2004 - 1. Preis 1st prize

Entwurf Design
Meinhard von Gerkan und Stephan Schütz
mit with Nicolas Pomränke

Projektleitung Project Management
Nicolas Pomränke

Mitarbeiter Entwurf Design Staff
Clemens Kampermann, Sophie v. Mansberg, Li Ling

Mitarbeiter Ausführung Planning Staff
Clemens Kampermann, Annette Löber, Li Ling, Lin Wei, Thomas Krämer, Johannes Erdmann, Kian Lian, Gerd Meyer, Helga Reimund, Chongsong Dong, Xin Meng, Jochen Sültrup

Freiraumplanung Landscape Planning
Rehwaldt Landschaftsarchitekten

Chinesisches Partnerbüro Chinese Partner Practice
ECADI

Akustik Acoustic Engineering
Müller BBM

Bauzeit Construction Period
2005–2010

BGF GFA
insgesamt in total 80.000 m^2

Opernhaus Opera Hall
1600 Sitzplätze Seats

Konzerthaus Concert Hall
1200 Sitzplätze Seats

Multifunktionssaal Multifunctional Auditorium
400 Sitzplätze Seats

Hotel Hotel
300 Zimmer Rooms

Musikinstrumentenmuseum
Museum for Musical Instruments
4000 m^2

Konferenzzentrum Conference Center
3000 m^2

Bildnachweis Picture Credits

Christian Gahl
Titelmotiv Cover
Seiten Pages 6–7, 34–47, 52–56, 60, 64–71

Hans-Georg Esch
Seiten Pages 49, 50–51,57,58–59, 62–63

gmp Archive
Pläne, Zeichnungen und Visualisierungen
Plans, drawings and visualizations
Seiten Pages 48, 51, 59, 61

Yuan Ying
Visualisierungen
Visualizations
Seiten Pages 12–13, 16–23

Ullstein Bild
Beispiele - Opernhäuser weltweit
Opera Houses–worldwide samples
Seiten Pages
24 ullstein bild – Iberfoto/Raga
25 ullstein bild – imagebroker.net/fotosol
26 ullstein bild – Prisma/Raga Jose Fuste
ullstein bild – Keute
27 ullstein bild – Lineair/Flavio Varricchio
ullstein bild – Schöning
28 ullstein bild – Raimund Franken
ullstein bild – CARO/Thomas Ruffer
29 ullstein bild – CHROMORANGE/TipsImages/Andre
30 ullstein bild – imagebroker.net/Ralph Kerpa
31 ullstein bild – Konzept und Bild

ON Grafik – Hamburg
modifizierte Welt- und Chinakarte
modified World and China Map
Seiten Pages 8–9

Impressum Imprint

Konzept Concept
Michael Kuhn gmp
Leiter PR und Kommunikation Head of PR

Herausgeber Editors
Meinhard von Gerkan gmp
Stephan Schütz gmp

Koordination Editing Direction
Claudia Tiesler gmp
Xiaoshi Fang gmp
Shan Shan Zheng, Peking gmp

Layoutkonzept und Satz Layout and Typesetting
ON Grafik – Tom Wibberenz mit with
Hendrik Sichler, Hamburg

Lektorat Proofreading
Philipp Sperrle (dt.),
Inez Templeton (engl.)

Übersetzung Translation
Hartwin Busch, Ashdon, UK (en.)
Christian Brensing, Berlin (en.)

Bildredaktion und -bearbeitung Picture Editing
Trixi Hansen gmp
Guido Brixner gmp

Reproduktion Reproduction
DZA Druckerei zu Altenburg GmbH

Druck und Bindung Print Production and Binding
DZA Druckerei zu Altenburg GmbH

Papier Paper
Multi Art Silk von by Papyrus Europe
150 g/m²

Schrift Font
Linotype Avenir Next Pro

Titelmotiv Cover Picture Christian Gahl
Bibliografische Information der Deutschen Nationalbibliothek
Bibliographic information published by the Deutsche Nationalbibliothek
Die Deutsche Nationalbibliothek verzeichnet diese Publikation in der Deutschen Nationalbibliografie;detaillierte bibliografische Daten sind im Internet über http://dnb.d-nb.de abrufbar.
The Deutsche Nationalbibliothek lists this publication in the Deutsche Nationalbibliografie; detailed bibliographic data are available on the internet at http://dnb.d-nb.de

jovis Verlag GmbH
Kurfürstenstraße 15/16
10785 Berlin

www.jovis.de

ISBN 978-3-86859-321-1